S0-DLQ-710

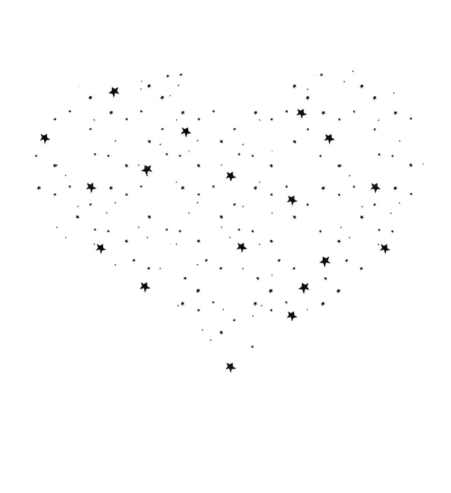

off to see pub.

this book is for you
please write, draw,
create, color, make lists,
or anything
that makes you happy

it's in back & white
so you can decide any
colors or shades of grey
you want to bring to it:
in thought, in writing
or in any way you wish

this book is for you

and for my mom
and for my son, my sun

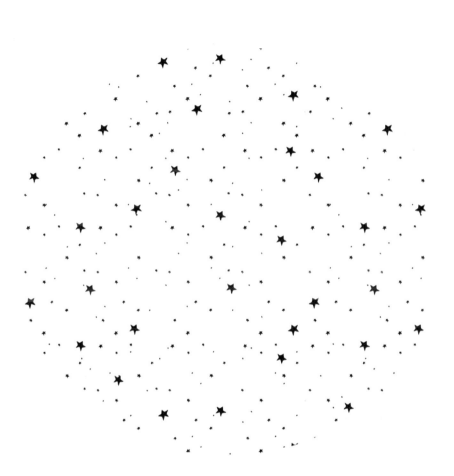

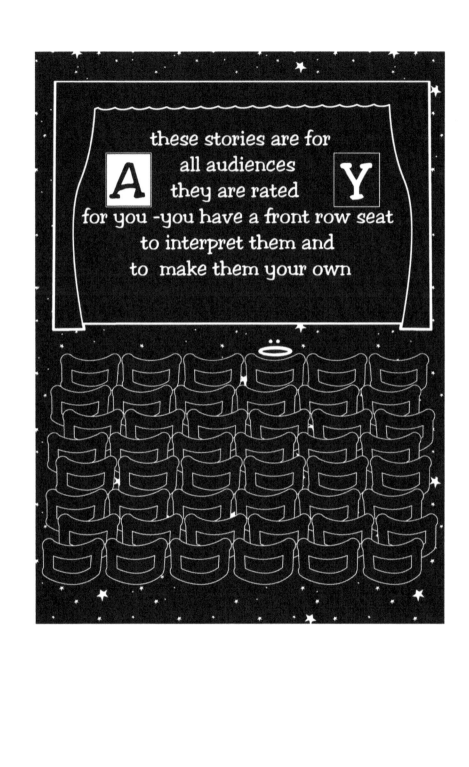

these stories are for
all audiences
they are rated
for you -you have a front row seat
to interpret them and
to make them your own

A

Y

every star a wish
every day a hope
every cloud a dream
every life a love
every door a window
every friend a smile
every laugh a light
every scraps of life

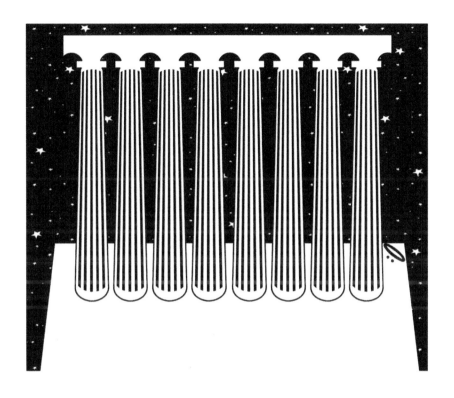

sometimes all we need
is a good foundation

she wanted her message to make a splash

healing isn't linear

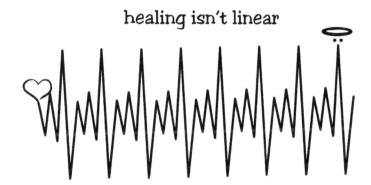

but it is strong and steady and from the heart

it was fine in the sky,
but not in his head -
he couldn't let
the spirals and circles consume him

circular thinking can be consuming, exhausting - can you think of some great distractions if it happens to you?

every notes
every memories
every loves
every friends
every secrets
every hopes
every wishes
every things
every dreams
every days
every nights

it's what's underneath that counts

even when things are inside out.
upside down or sideways
home is where you hang your ~~heart~~ hat

very long ago,
the walls appeared
so fast, she hardly
even noticed them.

at first she felt
safe behind them:
sheltered, certain,
protected, content.

but as she grew,
they chafed a bit.
what would it be
like without them?

she wanted to see the other side, so one day,
she removed a brick - just to take a peek.

then cautiously and only at her own pace,
she removed a brick at a time

every notes
every memories
every loves
every friends
every secrets
every hopes
every wishes
every things
every dreams
every days
every nights

what walls have you built? are there any bricks you could remove from the wall?

the darkness was scary and heavy
and the unknown more terrifying,
but when the knock of friendship came,
courage beckoned him to open the door

he was glad he'd done it
he felt lighter with a friend's encouragement -
even when occasional shadows revisited

every notes
every memories
every loves
every friends
every secrets
every hopes
every wishes
every things
every dreams
every days
every nights

what do you love
?

i shall be telling this by and by
somewhere ages and ages hence:
two roads diverged in a life, and i -
i took no road to travel by,

and that has made all the difference.

some things sooner,
some later,
but you can definitely
figure it out

there are certain things she would
never give up no matter her age or maturity,
no matter life's ups and downs -
they were things
that had no equivalent as she grew.
her favorite was a blanket fort
she shared with a friend

being a child should be a happy simple time
(not that it is like that for everyone) - but it
represents a joyful, learning, and playful place
in life. you're never too old or grown up to explore
that peace. what could you do to enjoy yourself -
for a moment, an hour, a day or longer?

every notes
every memories
every loves
every friends
every secrets
every hopes
every wishes
every things
every dreams
every days
every nights

no shoes too big to fill

it wasn't a trick. it was just who she was:
she tried never to make anyone feel small
she worried they could disappear

there's a lot to be said
for taking it slow

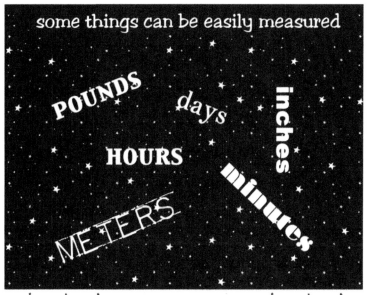

some things can be easily measured

POUNDS   days   inches

HOURS

minutes

METERS

some things can't

family   caring   acceptance

KINDNESS

FRIENDS   love

what's most important?
you are

she found it relaxing
to cast and see what surfaced

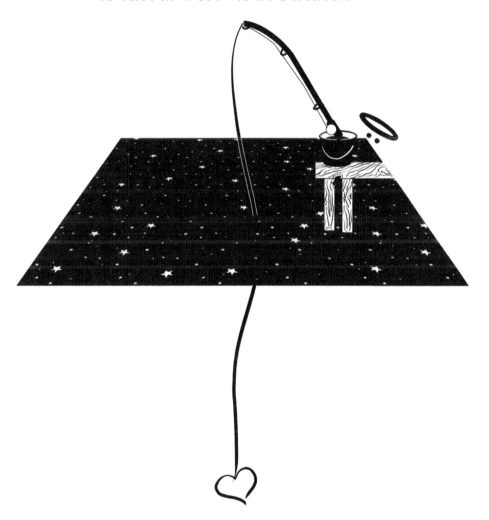

what makes you happy - today - right here & now?

every notes

every memories

every loves

every friends

every secrets

every hopes

every wishes

every things

every dreams

every days

every nights

he knew eating right was important

there are friends
and there are best friends

and then there is
the greatest friend ever

a bit of sugar and a bit of spice.
makes everything a little nice

keep your eyes on the road -
you never know who you will meet on the journey

the vacation page
where are the places you'd like to go, things
you'd like to see, wonders you can visualize?

every notes

every memories

every loves

every friends

every secrets

every hopes

every wishes

every things

every dreams

every days

every nights

counting them didn't really help him sleep
but he liked to start his rest that way
he gave each one a worry
to take as it leapt away

yawnnnn - what makes you calm and relaxed?

every notes
every memories
every loves
every friends
every secrets
every hopes
every wishes
every things
every dreams
every days
every nights

give yourself a gift

past....... .....future

put history in it's place
and have the best today

they loved their job - a balance -
it was breathtaking work all the time

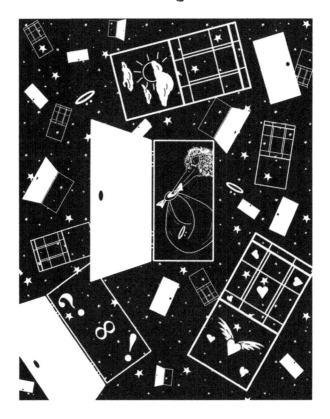

and an honor - safekeeping
the opening and closing
of all those doors and windows

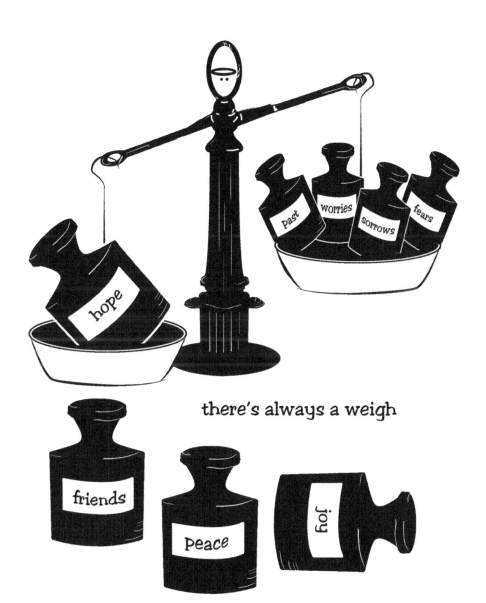

there's always a weigh

the cloudhopper loved his job -
pretending the clouds in the skies
mirrored the storms of his past

soaring and gliding far above them,
he let the winds do their thing,
taking him where they would

there were times it seemed easier
to bury her thoughts and feelings
to get through the day
as automatically as possible

what is the most **FUN** thing you could do right now?

just breathe

there were days he felt he could speak,
a place he felt safe and neutral,
people he felt he could trust -
the important thing was setting limits,
because too much talk could weigh too heavily

some things in life are
   gone
      but not forgotten

in some cases
      that's really okay
   and in others, forgetting is even better

she'd decided that talking to people
was as unique as buying presents for people -
large, small, more, less
so much to consider

because speaking heart to heart
was truly a gift

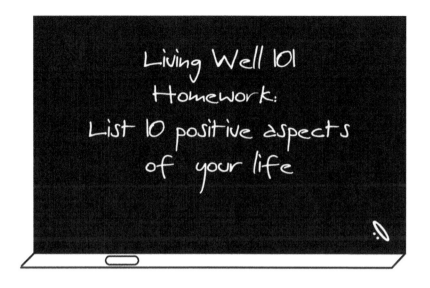

he liked to learn new things -
any kind of new things

it helped keep his mind off of old things

"we learn something new every day"

every notes

every memories

every loves

every friends

every secrets

every hopes

every wishes

every things

every dreams

every days

every nights

what did you learn today? what could you
learn tomorrow?

at first she could only remember
when the bicycle fell so long ago -
it hadn't been her fault,
but she felt consumed
by the injuries, fears, and pain

now, though, she hardly recalled it,
unless she noticed the long faded scar

and it felt freeing to ride in the winds again

a director knows many wise things -
the most important is when to take action

this is the page for action. do something
right now, no matter how small or large,
just do one proactive thing
you know will make your life better.

there were things he could accept -
then there were the unacceptable.
those things he couldn't change
that stormed around him from time to time

fortunately,
he could control his umbrella
for shelter

she knew some things in life were fair

for others she knew she had
to go along for the ride -
whether or not it was smooth

sometimes she found help
in the oddest of places

every notes
every memories
every loves
every friends
every secrets
every hopes
every wishes
every things
every dreams
every days
every nights

it can take a lot of trust to ask someone for help.
maybe this page could help you start small
by finding tiny tasks to test the waters.
who do you trust with what?

when she rose and didn't panic,
she just paused,
stopping to realize time and space
had grown within her and
the seed of hope had bloomed

she often didn't mind being alone,
she could spread her wings and soar

it had been so long, but when they
saw each other on the corner,
it was like nothing had changed -
still the best of friends

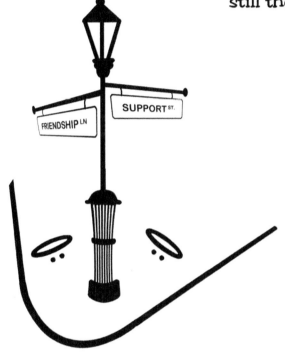

but as they renewed their acquaintance,
they knew it was more than randomness or luck

they'd each been through so much

what could you ask of the people in your life
to feel more supported? and/or what limits could
you set to feel more at ease?

from time to time,
she would find a missing piece

after a time, she knew
she was whole again
and the pieces were just
shinier and more polished

as she turned the pages,
 things just looked brighter and brighter

she'd never thought it would really happen,
even when they told her it would get better

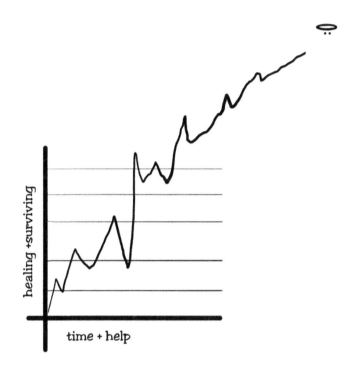

but lately, she felt off the charts

this is a place to reward yourself. you can draw yourself a medal or a trophy, list things you could give yourself as gifts or rewards and anything that reaffirms your greatness

every notes
every memories
every loves
every friends
every secrets
every hopes
every wishes
every things
every dreams
every days
every nights

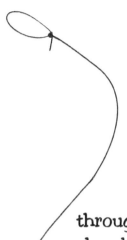

through ups and downs,
she always spun to safety
because of the helping hand

home
was where
she kept it -
always close

sometimes,
the more she searched for answers,
the more questions she found

sometimes there are no answers,
and if there were, they may not change things.

every notes

every memories

every loves

every friends

every secrets

every hopes

every wishes

every things

every dreams

every days

every nights

what answers would you want and how do
you think they would change you?

as a best friend,
he knew he couldn't confuse
hearing with listening

she'd always been
a neat and
orderly person

even after the chaos,
she attempted
to put things
where
they
belonged

people talk a lot about taking steps - how hard

the first one can be. take a step right here on this page any time

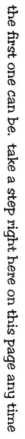

every notes
every memories
every loves
every friends
every secrets
every hopes
every wishes
every things
every dreams
every days
every nights

sometimes it felt alarming,
but she knew no matter what direction she chose,
hope and healing would come in time

perception and stereotypes
   lead to strange results

he actually had everything
he could ever want or need, and more

he just happened to enjoy
having his morning coffee
with a pen and pad,
drawing the beauty around him

i know you are special and unique;
what are your favorite things about you?

every notes
every memories
every loves
every friends
every secrets
every hopes
every wishes
every things
every dreams
every days
every nights

surviving is its own victory

surprise!

today and every day is your day
tonight and every night is your night
every star a wish, every day a hope
because you are your own miracle
celebrate you ☺

she couldn't have cared less
for most of the trappings,
but the shield,
the shield had purpose and meaning

a shield can symbolize your protection
what would be on yours?

every notes
every memories
every loves
every friends
every secrets
every hopes
every wishes
every things
every dreams
every days
every nights

so many signs
so many directions
take your own path
just follow the speed limit for safety

what makes
you feel
safe?

every
notes

every
memories

every
loves

every friends

every
secrets

every hopes

every
wishes

every
things

every
dreams

every days

every
nights

he used to feel terribly out of control
like the rushing waters would
take him under - turning tides,
coming in, going out, high, low, swirling

then he found a way to ride the waves

she kept her greatest treasure protected

this page is a safe place to write or draw anything you'd like.

every notes
every memories
every loves
every friends
every secrets
every hopes
every wishes
every things
every dreams
every days
every nights

sometimes we overlook the strength and safety
or forget the "little" things in our lives
until they reveal themselves or
we find
we really
need them.

he found the most ah-mazing journey-
he'd been lost for quite some time,
but now, he knew he could do it

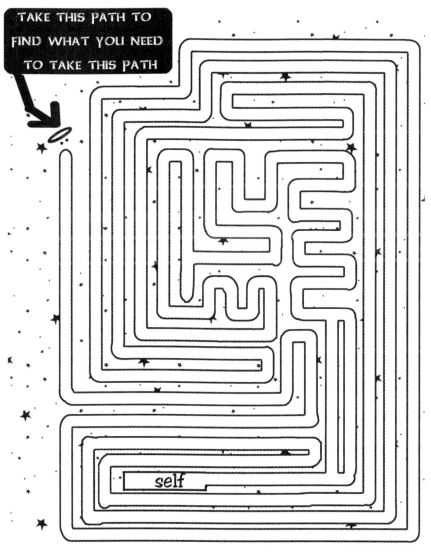

she imagined floating through starry skies
swooping by planets and moons,
and tossing away any problems
to be sucked away by black holes

TEAR HERE

the throw away page
if you want to put down scary, negative, angry.
or any other thoughts that discourage you, write
them here, then tear out this page, rip it into pieces
and throw it away forever

once she'd planted the seed,
    she watched it reach and grow,
        adapting, changing, bending -
            but never breaking

his favorite vision when he couldn't sleep,
was imagining himself when he was a child,
when things had not gone wrong yet,
feeling all tucked in and comforted
while the star watched over him

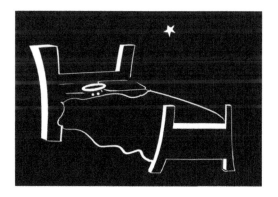

what makes you feel loved?

every notes

every memories

every loves

every friends

every secrets

every hopes

every wishes

every things

every dreams

every days

every nights

she had a sharp mind,
and she refused to be anyone's puppet

she made a list
just to see
who, what, how much, if . . .

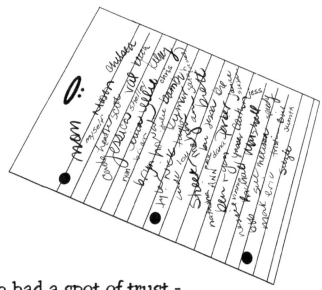

each had a spot of trust -

it wasn't all the same size
or even similar or the same parts -
but there were more of them
than she had imagined

every notes
every memories
every loves
every friends
every secrets
every hopes
every wishes
every things
every dreams
every days
every nights

what do you need to see in a person to
find a way to share and trust?

three cheers
for you,
the best cheer leader
anyone could want

so cheers to you
rah! rah! rah!

every notes
every memories
every loves
every friends
every secrets
every hopes
every wishes
every things
every dreams
every days
every nights

the positive page
a place for positive thoughts

a hidden side, doesn't make it a dark side

from no to full, slivers, quarters,
waxing, waning, yet constant like a good friend:
always there for reflection

people wear so many different hats,
    but friends take theirs off

there's no denying once upon a time,
she'd led a simpler life
when things happened to change that,
she withdrew - into a safe place
where she could think,
grow, heal,
become
more

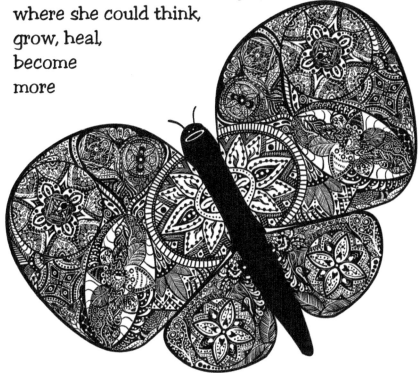

her emergence made her uncomfortable
she felt the complexity of what she'd been through
was written all over her where everyone could see

but we only saw her

affirm your awesomeness, because I KNOW you are

every notes
every memories
every loves
every friends
every secrets
every hopes
every wishes
every things
every dreams
every days
every nights

i know you can

    i know YOU can

whether she wanted to speak or shout,
even if she just wanted to whisper,
there was always someone there for her

she could test her words here for now
and see where that trust led later

she hated keeping
secrets. she felt like
she was always
on stage. was
everyone looking?
did everyone know?

it was her secret
to share - hers.
she should get to
choose how, when,
where, with whom.

she pictured herself leaving that pretend stage.
making a choice to join where she felt the most trust,
knowing she could feel safe, accepted,
knowing she could still change her mind,
knowing she could remain silent,
until she was ready to speak

every notes
every memories
every loves
every friends
every secrets
every hopes
every wishes
every things
every dreams
every days
every nights

what do you wish you could say?
here is a place to practice

every notes

every memories

every loves

every friends

every secrets

every hopes

every wishes

every things

every dreams

every days

every nights

united states
of
kindred spirits
make it your place
to be free and brave

it had taken her oh so many years
to realize she couldn't do it all on her own -
it had made her feel so small

now she realized
it took more strength to ask for help

exercise was good for her,
but she didn't choose the weights

she knew she could lift anything she chose -
because she was strong on the inside

Contacts

Exercise
Family
Favorites
Feelings
Friends
Fun
Guidance
Happy Things
Happy Thoughts
Happy Places
Healing
Help
Hope
Introspection
Joy
Loved Ones

Have a great day

whatever it takes, whatever you like
just take care of you

every notes
every memories
every loves
every friends
every secrets
every hopes
every wishes
every things
every dreams
every days
every nights

how do you
take care of you?

it's helpful to recognize when to fold
and when there's a hand to hold

why?

she decided that knowing
wouldn't change a thing for her,
so she made it be small and buried it -
understanding it would never
completely disappear

but it made sense to let
her world grow over things like this

there is always hope - always - what are your hopes?

every notes
every memories
every loves
every friends
every secrets
every hopes
every wishes
every things
every dreams
every days
every nights

she could glide through the turbulence
when she sailed on spirit

the safest place she could be

"Rawr!" he told her ,"
shout your courage to the world,
for you have survived, and now
you can thrive"

every notes
every memories
every loves
every friends
every secrets
every hopes
every wishes
every things
every dreams
every days
every nights

what brings you wonder and takes your
breath away?

they'd given her a great deal
of help and guidance,
so she set course
and found her treasure

shhhh - let's get a good night's rest

every notes

every memories

every loves

every friends

every secrets

every hopes

every wishes

every things

every dreams

every days

every nights

sweet dreams

wishing you well

every notes
every memories
every loves
every friends
every secrets
every hopes
every wishes
every things
every dreams
every days
every nights

every notes
every memories
every loves
every friends
every secrets
every hopes
every wishes
every things
every dreams
every days
every nights

every notes
every memories
every loves
every friends
every secrets
every hopes
every wishes
every things
every dreams
every days
every nights

every notes
every memories
every loves
every friends
every secrets
every hopes
every wishes
every things
every dreams
every days
every nights

"Hope" is the thing with feathers -
That perches in the soul -
And sings the tune without the words -
And never stops - at all -

And sweetest - in the Gale - is heard -
And sore must be the storm -
That could abash the little Bird
That kept so many warm -

I've heard it in the chillest land -
And on the strangest Sea -
Yet - never - in Extremity,
It asked a crumb - of me.

                                    - emily dickinson